Healing After a Breakup

A 50-Day Devotional & Guided INNER WORK Journal

By Dominica Applegate

Copyright © 2021

All rights reserved. No part of this book may be reproduced or transmitted in any form, by any means, electronic or mechanical, including photocopying or recording or by any information storage or retrieval system, without express permission in writing from the author, except where brief passages are quoted for the purposes of review.

rediscoveringsacredness.com

Commit to the healing path. Trust the process.

TABLE OF CONTENTS

How It All Went Down
The Ideal Ending
My Part in the Relationship Mayhem
The No Contact Rule: Necessary?
Grief as Medicine
The Pain Awakens Childhood Wounds
When You Can't Get Out of Bed
Self-Soothing
What Attachment Style Are You?
This Is How I Gave My Power Away
I Want What You Have
The Ho'oponopono Prayer
It Takes a Village
Clear Your Slate
Relationships as Mirrors
Help. This Fear of Abandonment Is Overwhelming!
Endings as Beginnings
Relationship Readiness
The Dating Blinders
Boosting Self-Esteem & Self-Worth
More of These, Please
Nix These, Please
Trigger Spotting
Safe, Secure Space for Growth
"We Need to Talk"

What Does Romance Mean to You?
Learning to Argue Well
The Longing to Feel Whole
Our Inner Lens
Internal Mind Shift
Explore Your Triggers
Getting Your Needs Met
What Do I Feel?
Think Turtle, Not Cheetah
Your Dream Life
I Am Not a Reject
Deal Breakers
Good Grief
You, Profiled
Who Do You See?
My Attachment Style
Life Vision
Me, Empowered
Dedicated To Authentic Love
And So It Is
One Step Back, Three Steps Forward
Onward, With Hope and Self-Love
What If I Don't Feel Better?
On A Positive Note
Celebrate Your Progress with a Ceremony/Ritual

INTRODUCTION

Connection.

It's something all humans crave.

Loss of connection, such as a relationship breakup, can trigger an emotional crisis where you literally feel like you will die.

Like you've been tossed into a pit of despair—trapped, wondering how in the world you will survive.

Alone.

One thing's for sure. Getting over a broken heart can be extremely tough. It can be heart-wrenching, dream-shattering, and destabilizing.

You may feel exhausted and your heart may literally hurt. You may feel angry, scared, sad, anxious, lonely, etc., — all these emotions colliding together.

Your heart may feel ripped to shreds.

If you're feeling like this, first I want to say I'm truly sorry you're experiencing this heartache. Getting over a breakup is a rough road to travel.

Second, I want you know that you are not alone. Many of us can relate to the emotional roller-coaster ride that follows a breakup. While knowing this may not make you feel better, perhaps this will:

Today, you can embark on an inner journey to turn this heartache into an opportunity, where you can:

Ø Do some serious soul-searching
Ø Rediscover who you are outside of a relationship
Ø Illuminate shadows that lurk in your psyche
Ø Let go of what needs to go
Ø Retrieve and polish parts of you that feel shattered
Ø Deal with any unfinished business from your past
Ø Grow and learn valuable lessons about relationships and life
Ø Become more self-aware, showing up for your own self, empowered.

Here lies a fork in the road.

One road will take you to VICTIMVILLE, full of people who didn't do any kind of inner healing work after a breakup. They numbed out, self-medicated, repressed the pain, made no effort, jumped into another relationship to numb their pain, etc.

The other road leads to EMPOWEREDVILLE, full of people who took the time to deal with emotional baggage, feel and heal the grief, break out of faulty belief patterns, and rise from the ashes like the phoenix ablaze with strength and wisdom.

What kind of path will you take?

I assure you that embarking on a self-directed inner healing journey during this time can help you reach EMPOWEREDVILLE, and that's going to feel a whole lot better than landing in VICTIMVILLE.

How Can Journaling Prompts Help Me Get Over a Breakup?

Journaling is a meditative tool that can help you release onto paper some of that pain you're feeling. It's a practice that can help you feel less overwhelmed emotionally.

It's also a judgment-free space where you can explore your thoughts and feelings. You can write whatever you want—the good, bad, and the ugly—without worrying what others will think or say.

Like when someone says, "OMG, will you just get over them already? Move onto someone else. There are plenty of fish in the sea."

It can feel disheartening when others are being so insensitive.

When you journal, no one can chime in with their ignorant or biased opinions. You can enjoy freedom of thought and speech. And that will feel great!

Not sure what to write about?

I've included fifty journaling prompts (questions) that can help you think about and answer growth-oriented questions, rather than solely focusing on how heartbroken you are.

Sure, it might feel like a tsunami has washed all your joy away. It may feel like you've taken a hundred knives to the heart.

I'm certainly not invalidating how you feel.

I'm holding your heart sacred right now, allowing you plenty of space to feel whatever it is you're feeling.

But hear me out on this.

At this exact time in your life, you have the opportunity to do some digging to learn valuable lessons.

Insightful questions can help you heal and evolve beyond old, worn out, faulty patterns that may be landing you in the same type of relationship that doesn't serve you or won't last.

Many of us have thoughts, belief patterns, unresolved trauma, old wounds, faulty internal programming, etc., that ultimately cause our relationships to tumble one by one.

No matter how much we think, *This is the ONE*, we find ourselves crying the breakup blues sooner or later.

It's certainly disheartening.

But today, you can wipe your slate clean and embrace a fresh outlook. Let the past stay there and commit to a new chapter with a new perspective.

You may be thinking, *But I'm hoping maybe my ex and I can get back together.*

I understand that thought all too well.

But here's the thing.

Whether you do or don't get back together, make this "in between" time...

...SACRED.

Step up and focus on YOU. This can be a life-changing time for you, where you learn valuable life lessons that help you throughout life.

Make a commitment to do your "inner healing work," reclaiming any parts of yourself you've lost along your life journey.

It's time to feel what needs to be felt and heal what needs to be healed.

Get Ready to Go on an Inner Journey

I've included three helpful sections to introduce you to your journey:

1. Inner Inquiry

Inner Inquiry can help you work with any dense or heavy energy that's trapped in your body.

You know, those emotions you've repressed, stuffed down deep, numbed, disconnected from, etc. You may think they disappear, but actually, they stay lodged in your body.

Ultimately, you want to release those emotions bit by bit. I've included four questions that you can ask yourself as you navigate the many emotions you may be feeling right now.

2. Exercises to Help Calm Anxiety/Regulate Your Nervous System

Chances are you'll be contending with your fair share of anxiety after a breakup. These sensations can feel overwhelming. I share various exercises and techniques that you can use to reduce anxiety and regulate your nervous system. **They will come in handy**, especially in the days, weeks, and months after a relationship breakup.

3. The Grief Process

I've included a short section on the phases of grief, as learning about the grieving process can help you understand why you're feeling the way you do and give you hope.

How to Use This Journal

Each day, for fifty days, I briefly share insights and encouragement on a variety of topics, including grief, self-care, conscious relationships, attachment styles, coping, love, emotional healing, and more. You can read one a day or more if you choose.

Then, there are journal prompts (questions) to get you digging. Some of the prompts are about you, and others are about your ex.

Some prompts help you dig into your past a bit to see if you're carrying some negative coping mechanisms into your present life that are tripping you up.

I suggest doing one prompt per day, working at a mindful pace.

Make this a sacred act.

Light a candle, burn some sage or incense, and gently do this type of healing work with a great deal of compassion and self-love.

From my process of writing to facilitate healing, I have created these unique writing prompts to help others begin the grieving, digging, and healing process.

The questions may help you:

- Understand better why your relationship ended
- Accept and honor the "no contact" rule
- Come to know what some of your blocks were
- Begin working through the phases of grief
- Begin to move through fear
- Let go of the need for closure
- Learn what your "attachment style" is
- Recognize relationship patterns that are repeatedly kicking your butt
- Know what to do when you are ruminating on your ex
- Learn how to express emotions in a healthier way
- Discover lessons that can help you in a future relationship

I understand first-hand the despair, pain, and fear associated with the end of a relationship or divorce. More than once, I've curled up in the fetal position feeling like I was going through drug withdrawal.

It's not fun.

It's easy to think you will be swallowed up by such emotions or that life will never be the same. It's easy to want to repress, run, escape, numb the intensity of the pain, or jump into another relationship.

(Not recommended.)

They say healing takes time, and it does. But if time were all that was needed for healing, everyone would completely heal sooner or later, right?

If only.

Time does help. That's for sure. But it's also helpful to educate yourself some on how you can get through the dark night of this ended relationship in a way that ultimately helps YOU grow.

Be willing to roll your sleeves up, put your work boots on, and get to digging under the surface doing what I call "inner healing work."

NOTE:

Journaling can be helpful, but it's not going to magically heal a broken heart overnight. There are MANY factors that come into play when grieving the end of a relationship and moving on.

However, I do believe taking the time to answer thought-provoking questions and journaling can certainly help speed up the healing process. And, you get to really know yourself on a deeper level.

It Takes Two to Tango

It's easy to point fingers and solely blame the ex for everything. And there are certainly circumstances where the ex is the cause of most of the issues.

However, typically both partners play roles that contribute to a breakup.

For example, if Sally and Joe break up because Joe is verbally abusive and refuses to address his drinking problem, Sally has the right to point fingers. Joe's got major "issues" and that's not her fault.

But this doesn't mean Sally can't take time to do some digging to work on healing her wounds or rediscovering herself outside of a relationship.

She can learn about her internal and external boundaries, do some investigating to see if she's fallen into this type of relationship pattern before, gain insight to see if she was an enabler, learn about red flags, discover her attachment style, and more.

For the sake of your inner healing, most of the journal prompts are geared toward helping YOU embark on your own self-discovery journey as you process and work through the pain you may be feeling at this time.

Work slowly through the writing prompts. Go at your own pace and really get in there at a deeper level.

1. Inner Inquiry

As you write your answers to the journal prompts, you're bound to feel various emotions surface. Everything from panic to rage to frustration to depression—and more.

A popular phrase in the mental-health field is "You have to feel to heal."

While it's true that feeling can be healing, if you're not sure how to handle those emotions that arise (or just repress them), you could find yourself flailing.

If you're anything like me, it can feel like anxiety will eat you alive at times!

As you work through the journal prompts, your task is to begin to **notice** what you are feeling and where you're feeling it in your body.

I'm going to say it again, because this is important:

- Begin to NOTICE what you are feeling

- And WHERE you are feeling it in your body

But I'm overwhelmed! I'm panicking. I'm enraged! I'm hurt! I'm depressed and feeling paralyzing aloneness.

You want me to FEEL that?

This is what you may be thinking.

And, I get it. I stuffed negative emotions down for many years.

You may feel so overwhelmed at times that you feel like it is too much.

You don't want to feel it!

Your mind races with thousands of thoughts, fears, etc. Your body may constrict, muscles tighten, ready for battle.

Or, your body collapses—immobilized, waving the white flag.

When we don't understand what's going on under the surface (in the psyche and/or body), it can certainly feel overwhelming.

The degree of panic, abandonment, fears, anxiety, etc., that's felt after a breakup varies from person to person. However, regardless of the degree of overwhelm, depression, panic, etc., learning how to track bodily sensations is your ticket to moving through and decreasing the intensity of these emotions.

This helped me incredibly, and I believe if you take the time to do this, it will help you too.

Become a Sensation Detective

What do I mean by "track bodily sensations"?

Think of yourself as a "body sensation detective." You're going to start viewing emotions and body sensations as a curious detective tracking them down and interrogating them in a "friendly cop" manner.

From a biological perspective, this process is called interoception, or the way we perceive how we feel based on sensations in the body. It's the awareness of what's going on **IN** the body at any time.

When you feel hungry or thirsty, that's you tuning in to bodily sensations. Your stomach growls. You notice it. You feel it (the sensation), and you go grab some food.

You feel like you have to urinate (sensation), and you head to the bathroom.

Easy, right?

But we can also use interoception during the times we are highly anxious or experiencing overwhelm of any kind, such as after a breakup.

And, we can use it to our advantage, rather than letting uncomfortable or overwhelming sensations cause us to feel like we are "losing it" or "can't handle it."

So, as you navigate this time in your life going through all the emotions that are common after a breakup, be open to becoming a "body sensation detective" and know that as you do . . .

. . . YOU ARE OPENING UP TO A NEW WORLD OF FEELING AND HEALING.

Regularly scanning your body and tracking sensations can help you better manage whatever emotions are wanting your attention.

Sensation Detective Practice

For example, let's say you get home from work and you plop on the couch. You've been in "work mode" all day and made it through the day without losing it emotionally.

But now as you sit on the couch, the silence and stillness triggers anxiety.

A lot of anxiety.

You mind starts churning with questions, fears, thoughts, etc.

- *How am I going to make it?*
- *I miss them so freakin' much*!
- *No one is ever going to want me.*
- *I can't handle this*!

Now, normally you may start freaking out. You cry, scream, yell obscenities at your ex, call your best friend to vent, or maybe head to the kitchen for a beer to calm the nerves. (Or whatever it is you do to try to calm down.)

But maybe you can try a new routine. When the mind starts racing, make a "time out" sign with your hands.

Pause.

Put on your "Sensation Detective" hat. Close your eyes and take two long, slow breaths.

Do a little investigating:

1. How am I feeling right now?

Drop within to do some investigating. Do your best to identify the sensations you're feeling in your body.

Is your heart racing? Breath shallow? Muscles tense? Shaking? Pins and needles? Energy flowing?

2. Where do I feel these emotions/sensations in my body?

Stomach? Chest? Neck? Everywhere? Nowhere?

3. If you can identify the emotion, name it out loud.

If you can't, that's alright. Just keep noticing where the sensations are in your body.

For example,

- "I feel you, anger. I feel you right there in my stomach."
- "I feel you, anxiety. I feel you right there in my chest area."
- "I feel you, depression. I feel you right there in my gut."

It may feel like the emotion(s) will overtake you.

You may feel like you're losing all control. I assure you, though, that if you consistently drop within, get familiar and connected with your body, you can learn to increasingly identify and feel these emotions/sensations without feeling like they are overtaking you.

It takes time and practice.

Slow down your breath, acknowledge the emotion, notice the sensations, and relax into them as best as you can.

This is where the technique of mindfulness can truly be helpful. Stay in the present moment, witness your emotions, embrace them momentarily, so that they can be processed and released.

4. Use visualization to release/integrate the emotions.

Then, take a slow, deep breath in and as you exhale through your mouth, consciously release that anxiety (or other emotion). You may want to visualize it melting (integrating) into your body. Or visualize the emotions releasing in whatever way works for you.

Use this four-step process daily. Use it when you begin to feel emotions stirring. Use it in the morning and before you go to sleep each night.

The idea is to stay present. Get firmly connected to your inner world and your body. Instead of allowing anxiety, stress, anger, fear, etc., to subconsciously control your life, you're CONSCIOUSLY learning how to feel, deal, and heal.

It helps.

This doesn't mean that negative emotions won't ever return, because some will from time to time.   Negative thoughts will do the same.

In fact, it's usually the negative thoughts that trigger the negative emotions. But when they do, know ahead of time that you're not going to repress them, run from them, or numb them.

As you practice this "noticing" and "feeling" little by little, you come to realize you can identify the emotion, feel it without letting it overtake you or freak you out, and let the emotion run its course.

This helps the emotion (energy in motion) GET OUT, rather than stay stuck in your psyche or body.

Exercises to Help Calm Anxiety | Regulate Your Nervous System

Believe it or not, a crash course in how the nervous system works can help you calm anxiety levels and heal past trauma and/or unhealed wounds.

Essentially, if you're feeling anxiety, your body has gone into "stress response" mode. After a breakup, our thoughts and emotions can trigger the nervous system to go into "high alert." It literally thinks a tiger is hunting us down for dinner.

For me, I was already contending with a lot of anxiety, as my nervous system leans toward the "dysregulated" side. Due to my unique childhood experiences, I had some "attachment issues" that caused me to fear abandonment.

At the threat of a breakup, or after a breakup, fearful thoughts would start racing and send my nervous system into a stress response that increased anxiety significantly.

Thankfully, I've learned ways to calm anxiety and better regulate my nervous system. It's a process. Trust me, the following techniques will come in handy if you apply them to your life. Try them out and see what ones work best for you.

Then, use them consistently to help you manage anxiety, fear, etc., and discover the already, ever-present peace that resides at your core.

4-7-8 Breathing Technique

Breathwork can help a lot when it comes to anxiety. The 4-7-8 breathing technique was developed by Dr. Andrew Weil. It's simple and it helps calm frazzled nerves.

- Relax your body.
- Breathe in through your nose to the count of 4.
- Hold your breath for the count of 7.
- Exhale through your mouth slowly to the count of 8.

Repeat three or four times and check your anxiety level. If you're still feeling quite anxious, repeat several more times. You can practice this breathing technique throughout the day to help your nervous system feel "safe."

Body Scan

Years ago, I had a friend that would always say to me, "You're all up in your head. Get into your body." At the time, I just couldn't figure out what she meant. It made no sense to "get in my body."

That was before I had a couple "Aha" moments where I realized I had a pretty big disconnect between my mind and body.

Essentially, I was "up in my head" listening to and ruminating on a thousand thoughts a minute, but never really "checking in" with my body. If I did feel an intense, negative emotion, I immediately stuffed it down deep.

Ultimately, this disconnect of mind and emotions caused me to feel depressed, numb, and anxious, all rolled up together.

Learning to do a "body scan" (and other body-work techniques) have helped me make a more solid connection between mind and body, reducing anxiety and tension.

This technique is easy. The toughest part is taking time to do it regularly. Essentially, you're going to lie down and "scan" your body with your awareness, progressively relaxing every muscle.

How to Do a Body Scan

Lie down, close your eyes, and bring your focus on your breath. Allow yourself to breathe naturally. The idea is to mentally scan your body from head to toe, purposely relaxing each section/area, taking note of any sensations you feel.

What do I mean by "sensations"? Tingles, tenseness, itching, numbness, heat, etc. If your anxiety levels are high, you may feel strong sensations in your chest area, for example.

As you go about your scan, be curious. Whatever sensations you notice in your body, stay neutral to them. You simply want to observe, take mental notes, and relax the entire body section by section. If your attention wanders, gently bring it back to your breath.

If you're scanning and feel uncomfortable sensations in your chest area, notice them. Try not to resist them. Take several slow, deep breaths and then move onto an area that feels better. Notice how your feet feel warm. Or your arms feel light, and so on.

I suggest doing at least one body scan per day. You can do this exercise whenever you want, but it's a great way to relax after work, wind down before bed, or use if you're beginning to feel intense anxiety, fear, etc.

When I first started the practice of body scanning, I had a tough time identifying what I was feeling in my body. I'd spent decades in emotional "shut down" mode. I reached out to a Somatic Experience therapist and this has helped me quite a bit.

Somatic Experiencing® (SE) is a body-centered therapy that focuses on helping people heal at the mind and body (somatic) levels. Dr. Peter Levine, a leading trauma therapist, developed this type of therapy more than forty years ago and it has proven quite effective. It's worth exploring.

"Voo-ing"

This anxiety reduction exercise is similar to the way Sufi's chant the sound "om," except here we're using the sound "voo."

This breathing technique by Somatic Experiencing® founder, Peter Levine, has helped me calm my nervous system many times. I have incorporated this exercise into my morning "nervous system regulation" regimen.

- Relax your body and take a deep breath through your nose.
- On the outbreath, gently make the sound "voo" and feel your belly and chest area vibrating.
- Take your time on the outbreath, continuing to "voo" until you're through exhaling.
- Pause for a moment and then inhale again slowly, automatically, repeating the "voo" sound on the exhale.

Stay present, mindful of what your body is feeling. You may feel sensations like tingling, vibrations, warmth, etc. Relax into them, as you remain present.

As you keep your awareness on the sensations and the vibrations, you're less apt to perceive them as uncomfortable, overwhelming sensations like you have before when your nervous system has become dysregulated.

Think of a foghorn that alerts you in the midst of thick fog to steer you in a direction where you can enjoy a safe, warm, loving home.

As you "voo," you're relaxing.

The sound vibrates the body in such a say that gives a message to the vagus nerve (part of the nervous system) that you are not in immediate danger, causing you to feel less anxiety.

Mindfulness

Mindfulness is an ancient technique where you bring your awareness to the present moment, while simultaneously observing and accepting any thoughts, feelings, or bodily sensations.

After a breakup, the mind can wander off with quite fearful thoughts.

- "What if I'm alone forever?"
- "This grief is going to kill me."
- "What if I can't make it?"
- "I'm going to grow old alone. I just know it."

Practicing mindfulness became a habit that saved me a lot of grief and anxiety. Rather than ruminate on the past or worry about the future, I started learning how to consciously be in the moment.

It made a difference.

Mindful living takes effort and practice. I downloaded a "Mindfulness Timer" on my phone that went off every fifteen minutes during the day. When the alarm rang, I would check in with myself to see if my mind was wandering or if I was consciously present at the time.

Usually, I was on autopilot off in lala land, so I would stop what I was doing and take a few moments to come back to the present. I focused on my breath and did a body scan. I purposefully relaxed and gave myself a big dose of love. I mentally told myself, "I am safe. I am loved."

I started taking "mindful showers." That was the first time in my life I was actually "fully present" while showering. I'd heard trauma expert Peter Levine share how this mindful exercise can help you reconnect with the body, part by part.

As the water would hit various parts of my body, I'd state out loud:

"This is my (hand, shoulder, hair, leg, etc.). This is my body. This is part of my body. Thank you for all that you do and for always showing up to do your part."

Use mindfulness to help you become more aware of the now. As you do, you may feel less intense negative emotions as you navigate this delicate time after a breakup.

Meditation

Meditation is a tool that can help reduce anxiety, stress, and other negative emotions. To practice meditation, you're going to sit or lie down and bring your awareness to the present moment. Think of it as taking time to be a "container" for whatever emotions or sensations are going on in the mind and body.

Here's how to do a simple meditation practice:

- Sit or lie down and consciously relax every part of your body.
- Close your eyes.
- Bring your attention to your breath.
- Take two or three slow, long breaths, relaxing even further.
- Feel how the air feels right on the tip of your nose as you inhale and exhale.
- Notice how your belly moves up and down.
- Continue focusing on your breath.
- If a thought comes (as thought are likely to arise), simply notice the thought with no judgment. Acknowledge it and then gently bring your attention back to your breath. The thought will dissipate.
- As you continue focusing on your breath, also pay attention to your body. Note any sensations without judgment. Do you feel tingling? Energy? Heat? Note the sensations. If you can identify what it feels like, mentally speak it.

Continue the practice as long as you desire. For beginner meditators, one minute might feel like hours. After all, the mind tends to race with a lot of thoughts.

As you become more familiar with meditation, you will slow down the thoughts. You can create space between the negative thoughts that have overtaken you in the past.

You'll learn to witness and release them, rather than be consumed by them.

As with mindfulness, meditation can help you learn to feel safer with uncomfortable feelings in the body, such as anxiety, worries, or painful memories.

Rather than "freaking out" or "numbing out," you progressively learn to acknowledge them from a distance (the observer), which tends to dissolve them.

Guided Meditations

Guided meditations can be quite helpful for reducing anxiety, fear, and other uncomfortable emotions. A trained practitioner uses their voice to gently guide you through the meditation. They may use visualizations, affirmations, etc., to help you achieve various goals, such as emotional healing, stress-reduction, etc.

There are many guided meditations on YouTube for all sorts of topics. If you're struggling with grief, anxiety, fear of abandonment, etc., simply do a search for the topic + guided meditation. I prefer to listen to them with headphones, but you can listen without them if you choose.

Try various ones to see what resonates with you better. If you find that meditating on your own is challenging, you may prefer guided meditations. Create a playlist for yourself of your favorites.

The Grieving/Healing Process

Grieving an ended relationship can resemble the grief associated with the death of a loved one. It's loss, and that loss can be paralyzing. It can feel like you've been abandoned.

The amount of grief you are feeling right now can vary depending on many factors.

Most of us can relate to feeling a wide range of emotions that surge through the body—anger, fear, sadness, shame, guilt, anxiety, and more.

Grief is a natural process that occurs after experiencing a loss. Embracing and working through, rather than avoiding, is the healthiest way to work through that process.

For many, grief hurts so badly that they go to great lengths to avoid feeling that pain. However, avoiding, numbing, addictions, or escaping it can keep you feeling stuck in anger, sadness, anxiety, rage, and more.

I'll briefly share now on five phases (or stages) of grief.

Keep in mind that sometimes the progress is not linear. You may get through Phase 1, 2, and 3, and then find yourself waking up one morning right back at number 1.

It's alright. Be gentle with yourself, as your process is uniquely yours.

As you progress through the stages, be sure that you:

- Surround yourself with friends and family who are supportive
- Commit to taking care of yourself (self-care)
- Take time daily to practice anxiety-reduction exercises
- Don't numb out with alcohol, drugs, or addictive behaviors
- Focus on this time to work on any issues you need to work on
- Reach out for professional help if you need

5 Stages/Phases of Grief

1. Denial (Shock) + Abandonment

It's likely that the first phase you'll encounter is shock or denial. You're in disbelief. The reality that this relationship is over may not have sunk in yet. It's surreal. You may have foreseen the breakup, even agree that it needed to happen. But still, you're having a hard time believing you can live without the person. That being single is your new reality.

Shock and/or denial are a normal part of the grieving process. This is a common defense mechanism that is trying to help shield you from some of the pain.

Along with shock, you may feel helpless, hopeless, and emotionally wrecked.

You may feel intense fear or panic. For many, a primal abandonment wound awakens and you may feel the weight of a lifetime of feeling alone, disconnected, rejected, insecure, etc.

It can feel like you're going through withdrawal, literally agonizing with intense longing for your ex. At the biology level, your brains have created an affinity for each other. You formed an attachment that has been severed with what may feel like a knife to the heart.

However, as miserable as you may feel right now, be encouraged that you can make it through such emotional overload. You ARE going to make it through, because you are willing.

You're more resilient than you think.

And, you're willing to "feel, deal, and heal" at a deeper level: MIND, BODY, and SPIRIT. You commit to trusting the process—one minute, one hour, and one day at a time.

Some stay here in denial for an exceptionally long time. This won't necessarily help. If you keep denying your grief or reality because it's just too painful, you could get stuck in this phase longer than necessary.

Be encouraged that this phase is temporary, albeit it can feel overwhelming at times. Actively commit to practicing self-care.

- Make yourself eat nourishing foods
- Get the best sleep that you can
- Reach out for support
- Nurture yourself

2. Anger

Anger is likely to come sooner or later. In fact, you may feel it at various phases or stages of the grief process. Remember, the healing path is a zig-zagging line and at times, you may loop back momentarily.

In this phase, you may wonder what in the world happened. You may be angry at your ex, at yourself, or both. You may even feel enraged.

Resentment may arise too. How dare they break up with you? How dare they do what they did? You're angry that they hurt you. You're angry that you must face life alone now. That you have to start all over with someone new.

You may become desperate to understand why and how. Why couldn't you two work it out? How did it all go south? You may become desperate in your mind, ruminating on the relationship, and trying to figure out all the answers. You want closure and you want it NOW!

Keep in mind that we can't always have closure. We don't always know the "whys." Sometimes we just have to accept the mystery and commit to taking the lessons we learn and applying them to the future.

You may be tempted to turn that anger inward toward yourself. Somewhere along your journey, you may have picked up this behavior.

Don't. **Decide to stop beating yourself up.**

Use this time to revamp and recreate yourself, using the emotion of anger as a steppingstone to a wiser, stronger, more empowered YOU.

Be on guard that you don't make any rash decisions during the anger phase. Sending harsh texts or emails to your ex is not recommended. Plotting revenge or hacking their social media accounts to post crazy stuff is not recommended.

Decide right now that you will do the necessary inner healing to WORK THROUGH the anger. Learn to express it in healthy ways, such as in therapy or journaling. Refrain from drinking or engaging in some other addictive or "numbing out" behavior as an attempt to not feel the anger. That simply won't serve you well and can make matters much worse.

Feeling angry after a breakup is normal. Those emotions arise for you to work through (feel, deal, and heal)—not run from or numb.

3. Bargaining

Somewhere along your grieving process, you may reach the bargaining phase. You may have had a couple weeks or a month of flying solo, but now you think maybe you want your ex back. Maybe it wasn't as bad as you thought it was. Maybe they are thinking about you and wanting to try again.

Or maybe you're feeling so much pain and longing that you think getting back together is the way to alleviate that pain.

So, you get busy strategizing how you can get your ex back. At the very least, you tell yourself that you two can be friends.

You tell yourself that it's possible to make it work. That both of you can work things out, even if you've fallen on your faces a hundred times.

You will figure out a way to get back in touch with your ex. You'll text them with a question. Send an email. Drop by to give them something they forgot at your house. Run into them at the grocery store you know they always shop at on Saturday mornings.

It may be terrifying to feel as alone as you may feel. You may feel like a dark abyss is going to swallow you whole at any moment. Such intense feelings can cause you to gravitate toward the past to try to find some security.

You may hope, wish, dream, figure things out, and promise to make it all better. You figure out what you did wrong. You figure out what they did wrong. You look at all your old photographs and remember the good. You conjure up in your head how good it can be again.

Don't get me wrong. Some relationships CAN be rebuilt and restored. Sometimes a "break" can help couples gain insight that helps them realize they want to try again.

I always cheer couples on that they can indeed heal, learn, and create a healthy, secure relationship.

I don't know what your situation is. The possibility of reconciling depends on various factors. But if your relationship is truly over (and you know this in your gut), bargaining behaviors may only prolong the acceptance necessary to move on.

4. Depression

It's normal to experience mild, moderate, or severe sadness or depression after experiencing the loss of a breakup. You may feel this simultaneously with the shock and anger phases.

I know I did.

After all, experiencing loss can shake us to the core. If you were abandoned, betrayed, or rejected, the weight can make life feel unbearable. Your sense of self-worth and security may feel completely shattered.

Keep in mind that some of these intense feelings could awaken old feelings of loss that perhaps haven't been "felt, dealt with, and healed."

For example, after a divorce, I encountered an avalanche of repressed negative emotions I'd stuffed down for many decades. It sent me to the deepest, darkest pits and I had no idea how to get a grip at the time.

Sure, those emotions had to do with the divorce, but they also had to do with a stockpile of pain I'd never processed and healed from childhood.

When you visit this phase, it's likely you've started to accept that it's truly over. You're starting to surrender, and it feels awful. You may feel depressed, disillusioned, frustrated, scared, and alone.

This is definitely a phase in which you will want to have a couple really good friends or a support system to help you through. You may want to spend some time alone, which is alright. It's a great time to go inside to reflect and contemplate. But you may also want to learn some tools that can help you begin to "feel, deal, and heal" the emotions associated with depression.

As with any stage/phase that feels too heavy to carry, give yourself permission to reach out for help from a counselor, support group, friends, etc.

5. Acceptance

Acceptance will come sooner or later. I know it may be tough to fathom now

It's likely to come incrementally. In its earliest form, it may be more like surrender. You accept that the breakup has occurred—not necessarily because you want to, but because that's reality.

You have enough awareness to know that reconciliation is not going to happen. You've accepted that you want to move on. You may still be licking some wounds, but you're determined to get on with your life.

You stick to the "no contact" rule and wave your little white flag. You may still hurt some, but it's less and less.

You may have better insights now as to what happened in the breakdown of the relationship. You may also be able to better own your part, applying lessons learned to any future relationship.

You may also find yourself offering forgiveness for yourself and your ex. Even if you don't "feel" it, making a conscious decision to forgive can help YOU as you move on.

Trust the grieving process and take the time to do some inner healing work. Make the effort to get to know yourself better during this time, learn more about relationships in general, and recreate YOU using the valuable lessons gained from "doing the work."

How Long Does the Grieving Process Take?

The best answer experts can give is, "It depends."

The time to progress through the phases of grief varies from person to person, based on different factors, such as:

- The length of the relationship
- How functional or dysfunctional the relationship was
- Coping skills
- Support system
- Whether you're making the effort to get through the phases
- Whether or not you're self-medicating with alcohol or drugs
- Mental and/or emotional health
- What attachment style you are

It could be weeks, months, a year, etc. You may get through the shock, anger, and bargaining phase and find you're right back to feeling angry.

You may embrace acceptance one day and the next you're back to bargaining behaviors.

Give yourself permission to work through the phases at your unique pace. At the same time, commit to learning more about relationships in general and doing any inner healing work you may need to do.

It will help you in the long run.

My best advice is if at any time you want or need support, find someone that you can reach out to that can hold sacred space for you to grieve and heal. A trusted friend, family member, therapist, pastor, healer, etc., can help tremendously as you navigate life after a breakup.

I will post resources and recommendations at the end of this book that can be helpful as you navigate this time in your life. Check them out as you progress through the journal questions for additional support.

Caution Against Numbing Out or Self-Medicating

Many people are tempted to deal with the tough emotions after a breakup by numbing out, escaping, running, self-medicating, etc.

Are you doing any of the following to numb out or escape?

Ø Drinking, abusing drugs, over-working, isolating, over-shopping, over-engaging in sex, gambling, over-eating, binge-watching everything, partying like there's no tomorrow, or another behavior.

Ø Are you repressing the pain and acting like everything is fine and dandy? {Shutdown Mode}

Numbing, running, and repressing may feel like it's the right thing to do. I understand it hurts so much, but these behaviors may very well cause you problems sooner or later.

Think of it like this.

Imagine yourself standing in an empty parking lot with a bag thrown over your shoulder (like Santa's bag of toys).

When you avoid dealing with tough emotions by repressing, rejecting, escaping, numbing, shutting down, etc., it's like you're placing bricks in your bag.

Day after day, if you're refusing to "feel, deal, and heal" that pain, you're adding brick after brick to that bag.

You may think you're "handling" the pain, but you're actually **accumulating baggage**. You're stockpiling dense, heavy energy that you carry day in and day out and likely right into your next relationship.

It won't serve you well.

So, make a commitment to refuse to self-medicate, numb out, or repress that pain.

Instead, get to doing your inner healing work so you can heal what needs to be healed, learn valuable lessons, and begin moving on with some optimism and helpful tools to start rebuilding yourself.

Now, let's get into the meat of this healing journal!

If you find you need more writing space, keep a notebook handy.

there's no easy fix

for healing pain.

feel it. honor it.

give it space

to be heard.

in doing so,

healing comes,

incrementally.

(1) How It All Went Down

Take a slow, deep breath and exhale. What are your feelings about how the relationship ended? Think back to the actual breakup day. List as many emotions as possible and don't hold back.

Notice how your body feels while exploring the feelings. Where do you feel them in your body? Stomach? Chest? Neck? What sensations do you feel? Heat? Pins and needles?

Feel the emotions, breathe through them, and allow them to flow through you. Relax into them rather than resisting, ultimately letting them go. If you start to feel overwhelmed, come back to focus on the breath, inhale to the count of 4, hold for 7, and exhale for 8 seconds.

i am so worthy

(2) The Ideal Ending

This question is applicable whether you wanted the relationship to end or not. Do you wish the actual breakup would have gone differently? If so, how? What would have been ideal for you?

Do your best to write this from a space of non-judgment. Try not to point fingers here. Simply write how you wish the breakup would have unfolded.

Before you start writing, take a slow, deep inhale and exhale. Do a quick body scan, relaxing into this present moment.

i believe in goodness

(3) My Part in the Relationship Mayhem

With huge amounts of compassion for yourself, state how you contributed to any issues in your relationship. Seriously, no self-judging here. Only conscious awareness of how you (your flaws, emotional immaturity, trauma responses, expectations, mistakes, traits, old wounds, the human being doing the best you can) contributed to "problems" in the relationship.

Deep breath in, exhale slowly. Here is an opportunity to start illuminating and owning your "shadow side."

focus on self-love today

(4) The No Contact Rule: Is It Necessary?

Relationship counselors will tell you going "no contact" is of primary importance in a breakup because it will help you be able to let go, tend to your own wounds, and eventually, move on. No calling, emailing, texting, etc.

When you reach out, you're stalling your "moving on" process.

But I want closure? You may not be able to get it, and that's alright.
But I think we can be friends. More than likely, you will not be able to be friends—at least not now.

Letting go and moving on is part of the grieving process, and going "no contact" is the best way to get started.

How do you feel about this? Intense inner pain? Agonizing loneliness? Fear? Anger? Get it out on paper.

i can do this

(5) Grief As Medicine

The first thing most people want to do at the end of a relationship is do whatever it takes to numb the pain. To somehow escape it because it can feel like a ten-ton truck crushing your chest.

But what if that grief can be medicine for unhealed wounds that started back in childhood? Help you come to know, love, and trust yourself at a much deeper, authentic level? What if it's a message, prompting you toward shedding what needs to be shed?

Today, write a short letter to your grief, but as a friend rather than foe. Let it know that you feel it coursing through your body. Talk to it. Ask it questions. What messages does it have for you? What do you want to say to it? Begin a dialogue with the grief you're feeling and trust that as you do, the process is indeed medicine for your soul.

i am trusting the process

I learned how to actually move on.
It didn't happen automatically.
I worried. I bawled.
I screamed into the abyss.
I missed *that* kind of love.
But I began doing "the work",
Becoming wiser.Braver.

stronger

dominica applegate

(6) The Pain Awakens Childhood Wounds

One time after a breakup, I sat curled up in the bathtub bawling like a baby. It felt like I was dying. I was shaking uncontrollably, feeling intense fear. I didn't understand at the time, but the pain of that breakup triggered some childhood trauma I'd never dealt with.

Namely, the fear of abandonment. It was as though all the unfelt pain of my lifetime showed up in real time to shake me to the core. Now I can see how I repressed emotions and "shut down," rather than feeling, dealing, and healing painful feelings. I'd never dealt with the fact that as a child, I felt neglected and abandoned by my parents.

You see, the residue (energy) from unhealed wounds or pain from the past doesn't disappear. It builds. That pent-up energy stays alive in the psyche and/or energetic body. And like a balloon that you keep blowing, it will eventually pop.

For many people, the pain of an ended relationship will be just the thing that "pops" the emotional bubble, allowing for the opportunity to tend to pain that's been avoided or repressed over the years.

Ask yourself, *Is there something from my childhood that's being triggered? Could I be dealing with unhealed wounds that are now activated? Could this be why it's incredibly overwhelming? Why I am paralyzed by terrorizing fear?*

{There's more writing room on the next page.}

keep doing the work

(6) The Pain Awakens Childhood Wounds

i am courageous

(7) When You Can't Get Out of Bed

It's easy to let self-care slide when you're struggling with so much pain. It's understandable to not want to get out of bed and tackle the days. Rest, but also practice self-care consciously.

Nourish your mind, body, and spirit regularly. Direct much of your attention to you. Yes, it hurts. Yes, you are in agony at times. However, when you practice self-care, you're growing stronger. You're boosting your self-worth. You're rediscovering who you are outside of an intimate relationship, finding your unique life rhythm.

Are you taking good care of yourself right now? If so, how? If not, why not? Make a list of things you commit to doing for yourself as you move on. Practice them regularly. Examples: affirming yourself, eating healthy, good hygiene, smiling, starting a new hobby, getting back to a hobby, creating goals, build a support system, etc.

i am a disciplined person

(8) Self-Soothing

Attachment theory experts state that about 50 percent of people grow up forming an "insecure" attachment with their primary caregiver. Without doing inner healing work to become more secure, this insecurity will carry over into the adult life.

This means that there are a lot of "insecure" adults walking around trying to enjoy "secure" relationships. Are you dealing with a lot of anxiety? What number would you give it intensity wise on a scale of 1-10?

Today, create your very own "self-love & self-soothing ritual" to help decrease the intensity of anxiety. Light a candle, burn incense, sage, etc., and get relaxed. Close your eyes and focus on your breath. Mentally repeat, "I am safe. I am loved." Other ideas include relaxing into a warm bath, repeating a soothing mantra, guided meditation, relaxing music, lie down and do an inner body scan, noticing the sensations in your body without judgment, absorbing the healing power of nature, ecstatic dancing, etc.

i am safe. i am loved.

(9) What Attachment Style Are You?

What kind of Attachment Style you identify with? There are four types:

Anxious—Higher anxiety, fears losing the relationship, craves deep emotional intimacy, anxious when separated, people pleaser, tough time saying "no," preoccupied with relationship, etc.

Avoidant—Quite independent, loves alone time, not a deep "feeler," walls around heart, shuts down, freezes when triggered, doesn't voice or realize they have needs, etc.

Both anxious and avoidant—Sometimes "Anxious" and sometimes "Avoidant," "I want you, go away," etc.

Secure—Low anxiety around relationship, trusting, interdependent, emotionally attuned, comfortable with intimacy, when triggered, responds rather than reacts intensely, etc.

Today, you have a homework assignment. Learn more about attachment styles and see which one resonates with you. Explore the topic and take notes. As you progress through this journal, knowing which style you formed growing up will help you continue to heal and grow.

i value security

(10) This Is How I Gave My Power Away

In every relationship, power dynamics are at play. A healthy relationship consists of two individuals who can stand in their empowered selves, staying true to what they want and need individually and as a couple.

A healthy relationship also involves two people who can help meet each other's safety and security needs. But sometimes this gets out of balance. How did you give your power away in the relationship?

- Saying "yes" when you wanted to say "no," primarily out of fear.
- You felt like a victim, having little to no control.
- You kept silent when you knew something was wrong.
- You let your partner do all the leading and decision-making.
- You were quite busy "people pleasing," putting them first.
- You lost touch with who you are, wrapping your world around them.

Write about how you can reclaim your power as a single person. And, how you can keep it in a future relationship!

i embrace my inner power

Right now, at this very time in your life, you have an opportunity to discover YOU in a real and raw way.

An authentic way that could shatter every mask you've lined up so neatly on your walls.

Amidst perhaps one of the greatest heartaches you have experienced lies a path toward self-discovery + inner wisdom + awakening.

At times, tread lightly. It's a delicate time.

Other times, dive deep.

Face the shadows that have been tripping you up.

It hurts and it's challenging and at times, you just want to say eff it and give up.

But don't.

Because bit by bit, hour by hour, day by day, you, dear soul, are becoming the "you" that through the years, you've forgotten.

The worthy, lovable, innocent, radiant, powerful...

...YOU.

Dominica Applegate

(11) I Want What You Have

When you met your ex, what did you see in them that you lacked? What attracted you to them physically and energetically?

Sometimes when we are energetically attracted to another, it's because we are sensing in that person things that we have lost or given away. It can also mean that they simply have strengths where we are lacking.

We can indeed complement each other in a relationship when it's operating at a healthy, secure level. But we don't have to chase others based solely on something that's underdeveloped in ourselves. Is it possible you did this? Tried to feel worthy based solely on their approval? Got with them just for security?

Explore the topic. Can you go within and cultivate some of those things yourself? (Security, worthiness, unconditional love, confidence, etc.)

(12) The Ho'oponopono Prayer

The Ho'oponopono prayer is a Hawaiian practice for forgiveness and balance. It's an intent or ritual that can help you openly express wrongdoing or pain that have occurred in your relationship.

It gives space for forgiveness and gratitude. Whether your ex, you, or both of you caused pain in the relationship, this prayer helps you own your feelings and experiences. It allows you to take responsibility for your actions. Pray this for you and your ex, if you desire.

"I am sorry. Please forgive me. Thank you. I love you."

What feelings arise as you pray this prayer for you? For your ex? Sit with these feelings and allow them to be heard and seen. Acknowledge them as a witness, breathing slow, deep breaths.

This is healing in the process.

i allow space for forgiveness + gratitude

(13) It Takes a Village

Navigating the weeks or months after a breakup can be rough. There may be days when you just need some support.

Do you have a solid support system in place that can hold space for you as you navigate this time of your life? Those that are compassionate? Patient? Encouraging? Who are they?

If you're lacking trusting friendships, how you can move forward with the intent to make a friend or two? You can also find valuable support by attending a support group (in person or online) or reaching out to a therapist, spiritual mentor, campus counselor, etc.

List your supports and how they are helping you.

i am staying on task. yay for me!

(14) Clear Your Slate

Self-forgiveness can help you clear your slate, so you don't have to keep carrying feelings of self-loathing. Most ended relationships aren't just the fault of one person. Usually, both partners have contributed to the dismantling of the relationship foundation.

Forgive yourself for your part. For those shadow parts of you that reared their heads. For the unhealed wounds from your past that erupted in arguments in the present. For mean thoughts, words, and/or actions. Don't beat yourself up.

Today, pretend you are a "Compassion Angel" and write a letter to you. Embody compassion and unconditional love and write whatever comes to mind regarding your behavior in this recent relationship and breakup. Stay focused on you and your part. Be gentle and kind, offering forgiveness and encouragement.

i am aligned with love

(15) Relationships as Mirrors

Often, relationships are mirrors that reflect back to us what we are feeling on the inside. In what ways did your ex mirror back to you how you were treating yourself?

When you can view relationships as mirrors, you can use them as a tool to achieve greater emotional healing and freedom. As you change your landscape on the inside for the better, you can attract those who will mirror back better. Keep making the conscious effort to change your inner emotional landscape for the better.

What did your ex mirror back to you that was going on inside of you? (Insecurity? Lack of self-worth? Lack of boundaries? Jealousy? Fear of abandonment?) Did your ex mirror back to you positive things? (Your inherent worth? Your beauty? Safety?)

my mind is quieting down

walk your own journey.
be unashamedly you.

(16) This Fear of Abandonment Is Overwhelming!

When the fear of abandonment arises, it's easy to do all sorts of things to try to get your ex back. Even if the relationship was toxic, it's tempting to text, email, etc., to see if that reconnection will calm the fear.

You may feel intense aloneness, desperation, and depression. Your nervous system is frazzled, dysregulated, and you may not understand why. However, you can work through the fear of abandonment. The activation of this fear is your opportunity to face it, feel it, deal with it, heal, and integrate it so that it will leave you alone.

How do you feel when this fear is activated? What specific emotions?

Where do you think this fear originated in your life? (Childhood? Teen years? Adulthood?) Are you really all alone in the world?

Write a short letter to this emotion of abandonment fear. Let it know that you will never be alone because you refuse to abandon yourself. Even if all the people in the world vanished, YOU have YOU.

(17) Endings as Beginnings

It's easy to feel like a failure when a relationship ends. Feelings of shame and disappointment can keep you stuck in the quicksand if you allow. However, ended relationships don't have to be viewed as failures. And YOU are not a failure just because your relationship ended.

Every ending offers a new beginning. Every ended relationship can be an opportunity to learn and grow in a variety of ways.

Do you feel shame or disappointment about the ending of this relationship? If so, why do you think that is?

If shame and disappointment arise, have a brief conversation with them. Acknowledge, witness, breathe through the feelings, and let them go.

Remind yourself of your positive qualities. Write them down right now. (Determined, cheerful, kind, insightful, honest, openminded, smart, confident, curious, creative, lovable, generous, etc.)

i am becoming more confident

(18) Relationship Readiness

A while back, I came across a short booklet about what to look for when you're searching for a long-term, committed partner. As I read through it, I noticed plenty of characteristics that I didn't see in myself. It was a humbling experience and caused me to dive even deeper into learning more about relationships and how I could show up as a better partner.

There were plenty of things about relationships that I'd just never learned growing up. There are also some wonderful teachers, counselors, workshops, and courses available that can help you no matter how little or how much you already know.

Did you have healthy relationship models growing up? Your parents? Grandparents? Other couples? What are some things you have learned about relationships? How will you apply these lessons to a future relationship? What does "relationship readiness" mean to you? How can you show up in the future as an amazing partner?

Willingness to "do the work" matters. It's not
always easy, but it is most certainly worth it.

(19) Dating Blinders

Were there any red flags in the dating stage of this relationship that you overlooked? If so, what were they?

Why do you think you missed them? Do you think you recognized them at a subconscious level, but went forward anyway?

Based on your past relationship patterns, what are the major red flags you will look for (and not ignore) should you decide to date in the future?

i am becoming more conscious

(20) Boosting Self-Esteem & Self-Worth

Many people beat themselves up after a breakup, solely focusing on the negatives, flaws, etc. While it's wise to own your part, it's also wise to focus on your positive qualities and what you added to the relationship.

What were some positive things you brought to the relationship? What did your partner love about you? What did you love about YOU regarding the roles you played or how you showed up in the relationship?

Keep those positive attributes and energies alive and well for yourself and the future.

i acknowledge my awesomeness

"You have the power to heal your life, and you need to know that. We think so often that we are helpless, but we're not. We always have the power of our minds...Claim and consciously use your power." Louise L. Hay

(21) More of These, Please

What do you miss about your ex?

As you write about these qualities and attributes, declare that you will enjoy the same and/or similar qualities in a future partner should you decide to enter another relationship.

In the meantime, how can you show up for yourself or allow others to offer you some of these qualities/attributes?

happiness is an inside job

(22) Nix These, Please

What do you NOT miss about your ex? Keep in mind you're not pointing fingers and blaming here. You are simply observing things that you really don't want showing back up in a future partner should you decide to enter another relationship.

Again, think about the Attachment Style you identified with. What Attachment Style do you think your ex was? Can you see how your differences contributed to the breaking down of the relationship?

This writing exercise may also help you remember why the relationship came to an end. The list might be longer than loneliness is letting you believe. And, this can help you from texting or emailing them just because you're feeling lonely. If moving on is your goal, keep this list handy to help you remember why the relationship has ended.

i am committed

(23) Trigger Spotting

What were some of your main triggers in the relationship? What were most of the arguments about? Can you spot a pattern? (Money, sex, jealousy, lack of communication skills, codependency, etc.) Did you struggle with some of these same triggers in previous relationships?

Conflict happens in every relationship, but what I want you to think about is how intense things got for you and/or your partner when you were triggered. There is responding and reacting. Then, there is over-reacting. Did your rational minds go offline? Brains get hijacked? Keep in mind that intense reactions to triggers can indicate unresolved or unprocessed pain or trauma from your past.

To increase your chances of not repeating negative patterns that aren't serving you, choose a self-directed inner healing journey or reach out to a therapist to work through old wounds. Shadow work, inner child work, and mind/body exercises are three great tools to get you going in that direction. You may also consider seeking a therapist who specializes in trauma therapy.

i am becoming whole

(23) Trigger Spotting

i am more aware of triggers

(24) Safe, Secure Space for Growth

A healthy, interdependent relationship involves two people who hold safe, secure space for each other. The foundation of relationships should be secure, because when we feel secure, we can relax and go about our lives freely with abundant energy. When insecurity abounds, we constrict and conserve our energy for "survival." That does not serve us well or feel good.

How were you at helping provide a safe and secure space for your relationship? How well did you know your partner? Did they feel secure? Did you?

As a team, partners can learn to help co-regulate each other's nervous system. It's not you versus your partner. It's both of you being individuals, but also teammates that can go to each other even with all your flaws, fears, etc., and find safety in the sacred space of that relationship. A secure, interdependent relationship can serve as a "safe space" for each person to be "all in." And, at the same time, venture out to follow their heart's desire, try new things, and learn valuable lessons.

Contemplate how safe and secure you and/or your ex felt throughout your relationship. What started breaking down that foundation of safety? Can you own your part? (If it applies.)

(25) "We Need to Talk"

How were your communication skills with your ex?

Did you find it easy to speak your truth to them? Or did you fear conflict when you communicated wants or needs? Do you think your ex felt comfortable communicating with you?

If not, why do you think that is?

Do you think you could use some help learning how to communicate more effectively? If so, what can you do to start learning? (Books, therapy, seminars, life coach, practicing, etc.)

i speak my truth in love

free to be

(26) What Does Romance Mean to You?

Most people agree that romance is a nice ingredient to have in a relationship. By romance, I mean feelings of love, an affinity for the other person, and various behaviors that express those intimate feelings. Were you romantic with your ex?

Did you take the time to stoke the fires of romance? Did your ex? Did the both of you sit and have conversations about intimacy and your love languages? Do you know your love languages? (If you don't, do a little research to find out.)

Did you have discussions about both of your wants and needs around romance? What are some key lessons you've learned about romance or intimacy based on this last relationship?

What does an ideal relationship look like for you in terms of romance and intimacy?

i am generous

(27) Learning to Argue Well

Many relationships end with plenty of arguments and intense emotions. It's not fun, and often, it's not pretty. Maybe you can't do much about your past relationship(s), but you can start preparing for a future one should you decide that's what you desire.

Arguing is not about winning. It's about coming together as a team, actively listening, and hearing each other. It's about offering empathy for whatever pain each of you are feeling. And, resolving conflict in respectful, healthy ways to ensure a more secure, safe relationship.

Take time to learn about what happens in your brain and nervous system when you get riled up. Learn more about "fight, flight, freeze, or fawn" mode. Learn some helpful conflict resolution exercises and practice them. Learn how to argue in healthier ways where conflict is seen, heard, and overcome in ways that ultimately bring you closer together.

How "well" do you argue? Do you tend to want to "win" arguments? Does your brain get "hijacked" and you lose it? How can you learn to argue in ways that ultimately strengthen relationships?

i am co-creating a good life

(27) Learning to Argue Well

i accept myself

(28) The Longing to Feel Whole

It's easy to feel like a partner will make you feel whole. Listen to love songs and many are about just that: finding a person who will complete you. However, one person cannot make you feel complete or "whole."

Yes, they can add value. Yes, you both can be in a wonderful "partnership." Yes, you can help each other feel some security. But if you're relying solely on them to complete you, you set yourself up for disappointment and hurt.

Did you go into the relationship thinking that person would complete you? If so, can you see where you gave some of your power away? Could this be one reason you're feeling such grief right now? What are some things you can start doing to feel more "whole" while being single? How can you nurture yourself mind, body, and spirit?

i am here to learn & heal

(29) Our Inner Lens

We often experience the world through an inner lens that we formed in childhood. For some, that lens becomes distorted with thoughts or programming, such as:

Ø I'm not good enough.   Ø I'm not worthy.   Ø I'm bad.

Do you feel this way? If so, it's time to tackle these misperceptions from various angles—mind, body, and spirit. Begin working with positive affirmations and/or shadow work daily to work with your mind. For your body and spirit, consider starting a mindfulness and meditation practice daily—plus some of the nervous system exercises mentioned at the beginning of this book.

Operating from our authentic inner lens takes practice. As you go about your day, remember to affirm yourself consistently. If you find yourself thinking something negative, affirm yourself out loud. This disrupts that neural connection, weakening it. Practice!

~~I am not good enough.~~ I AM GOOD ENOUGH
~~I'll never find true love.~~ I WILL ENJOY HEALTHY LOVE

i am non-judgmental

(30) Internal Mind Shift

More than likely, the breakup you have experienced has caused one or both of you immense pain. Depending on who broke up with who, you may feel that they are "the bad one" and you are "the good one."

Or vice versa. You may feel like a victim. Or, you may feel like an awful person if you are the one who ended the relationship. But what if this is far more than black and white. What if you could shift your mindset from victim/villain to a storyline where you can witness and acknowledge your ex's and your own quirks and imperfections without pointing fingers? Without rolling out the blame carpet? Without judging?

If you can't do this just yet, it's alright. But maybe you can aim for this non-judgmental storyline at some point down the road.

Contemplate and write a story about how you and your ex witness and acknowledge each other's imperfections or differences without blame. A neutral story that's marked with respect. Explore your feelings.

i can and i am

"When one door of happiness closes, another opens; but often we look so long at the closed door that we do not see the one which has been opened for us."
Helen Keller

(31) Explore Your Triggers

A trigger is something that sets you off mentally, emotionally, or physically. Reflecting on your past relationship, what triggered you the most? Common triggers may be getting yelled at, not being heard, being criticized, being told to do something, being ignored, etc.

Triggers often stem from past experiences that we've not quite worked out. That haven't been healed and integrated in the psyche and/or body. For example, if you were not heard in childhood and felt invisible, the pain from that wound (if not healed) can cause a big reaction if your current partner is not emotionally available or blatantly ignores you.

Triggers are tender spots in the psyche that if touched, can cause a reaction that goes beyond what is considered a healthy response.

List a few triggers today. Then, explore them. What put you in a tizzy? Caused a strong reaction? Track back to see if there may be some unresolved pain from earlier in life. Look for patterns and reactions. Commit to working through unresolved pain so it's less likely to show up in your next relationship.

As you discover your triggers, can you agree to become fully responsible for them?

If you find you can't work yours out on your own, consider finding a therapist who can assist you. It's well worth the investment.

___

___

___

___

___

___

i am determined

(31) Explore Your Triggers

just watch me

(32) Getting Your Needs Met

What is it that you are seeking from an intimate relationship? What are you needs and wants? Keep your Attachment Style in mind as you brainstorm. How can YOU meet these desires right now as a single person? Be as creative as you want.

As you identify your wants and needs, you can actively start meeting some of those needs now yourself, rather than looking "out there." If you can discover how to meet your primary needs, it can help you in that next relationship because you'll go in more secure and resourced.

Ø I need authentic connection. I will make a friend or two. I will get involved in a support group.
Ø I need to feel heard and understood. I will ask my best friend out for coffee once a week.
Ø I need to feel secure. I will keep doing my inner healing work, nurture myself daily, and reach out for emotional support as necessary.
Ø I need to feel peaceful. I am committed to a daily practice of . . . (mindfulness, meditation, prayer, yoga, nature walks, etc.)

what i want and need matter.

(33) What Do I Feel?

Some people deeply feel their emotions. They may even "overly feel" them, as in those that identify with an Anxious Attachment Style.

Others have a tough time feeling much at all, which is common for those that identify as "Avoidant Attachment Style." They may have largely disconnected from their emotions (perhaps in childhood) as a survival or coping mechanism in response to trauma or chronic stress.

Are you in touch with your feelings/emotions? Do you feel safe to feel them or do you "shut down" as soon as you feel those strong sensations in the body?

If you shut down, zone out, or have built a huge brick wall around your heart so you don't have to "feel," you may want to address this before getting back out there in the dating scene. This coping mechanism may have served you as a child, but it probably manifests "issues" in a relationship. (You're not emotionally present. I don't feel like you care. You're so cold, distant, etc.)

If you "overly" feel, and it causes you high anxiety, you'll also want to address this before getting back out there in the dating scene. It's likely your nervous system sort of got stuck in "survival" or "fight, flight" mode, and this can cause "issues" in relationships.

One type of therapy that works well for both Anxious and Avoidant Attachment Styles is called Body-Based or Somatic Experiencing therapy. Do a bit of research to determine if you'd like to pursue that route to heal unresolved trauma, learn to attune to your emotions, and express them in healthy ways.

Write about how in touch you are with your feelings. Do you "shut down" in an argument? Repress emotions? Have you ever been told that you're emotionally absent? Not present? Cold-hearted? Do you feel ultra-deeply? Have you been told you're "too emotional"? (No such thing, by the way.) Do you feel like your emotions overtake you?

I encourage you to be open-minded here and take time to explore this topic further.

(33) What Do I Feel?

i am learning so much about myself.

(34) Think Turtle, Not Cheetah

Assuming you one day may desire another relationship, note that there is no rush. Take some time to heal. But when you're ready to start dating, there are plenty of things to consider. For some, the anxiety that comes along with being single or alone can cause them to jump right into a committed relationship after one or two dates. They may ignore red flags.

Try not to do that. Long-term commitment IS a big deal. It ought to be a sacred choice. So, if and when you do get out there in the dating scene, take your time. Continue to work on healing any fears of abandonment, old wounds, trauma, etc. Allow time for conscious exploration of that person and the dynamics of the connection. See if they'll dig to see what their Attachment Style is. Do they lean toward Anxious, Secure, or Avoidant? What does it mean to partner up with an opposite?

This is a SACRED, CONSCIOUS exploration.

Have you rushed into relationships before? Or have you been rushed into a relationship? Today, make a declaration of your choice to go slow and steady like a turtle, rather than lightning-fast like a cheetah. List the benefits of taking your time in the dating stage.

_____
_____
_____
_____
_____
_____
_____
_____
_____
_____
_____

{There's more writing room on the next page.}

i am content

(34) Think Turtle, Not Cheetah

i am taking my time.

(35) Your Dream Life

Deep breath in, slowly exhale, relaxing. Today, take some time to focus and envision your dream life. Where would you like to be in three, five, or ten years? What kinds of things would you like to be doing? What are the primary emotions you want to be feeling?

Envision your future short- and long-term. This exercise is more about what YOU desire, rather than a future relationship. You may even want to make a "bucket list" and write down the things you'd like to accomplish. Brainstorm and let your imagination go wild here. Even if it feels super big, write it down anyway. You may or may not accomplish those things, and that's alright. Your life may or may not go as you desire, and that's alright. What you're doing is getting some creative energy moving and momentum going—and this can be quite beneficial on all levels. So, what's your dream life?

i am dreaming about so many lovely things

(36) I Am Not a Reject

It's easy to feel rejected when someone breaks up with you, or to reject yourself if you broke up with someone. Rejection is a feeling that throws us into "survival mode." At the nervous-system level, we literally feel like we are in danger—like a bear is about to eat us for dinner. This is a great survival mechanism if we're living in the jungle, but most of us aren't.

But just the thought of being a "reject" can signal "danger" . Think about those that lived in tribes way back. To be rejected meant they were out on their own to face the wild solo. And that did threaten their survival! So, a "warning mechanism" was developed to signal that they were about to be booted out of the tribe—namely, rejection.

While rejection may be something we all face in life in all sorts of situations, we don't have to allow that "survival" part to bring us down. We don't have to keep beating ourselves up in any way, shape, or form. If feelings of rejection come knocking on your door, remind yourself of just how wonderful you really are. Make a list of your best qualities you have to offer others, including friends, family members, co-workers, employer, and a partner. Build up your self-esteem and keep it boosted.

i embrace inner transformation

(37) Deal Breakers

Many people enter relationships without really knowing what their "deal breakers" are. Do you know yours? Deal breakers are those things that you have zero tolerance for in a relationship. They're those things that you firmly believe sever the connection you have with your partner. Something you have no desire to try to work through.

For example, common deal breakers are emotional abuse, physical abuse, sexual abuse (basically, abuse of any kind), infidelity, ongoing addiction with no effort to recover, repetitive lying, wants or doesn't want kids, etc.)

Think about what your deal breakers are for an intimate relationship. Keep in mind that these can change over time. And, there are various factors that come into play. (As in someone struggling with addiction, but is making the effort at recovery.) Knowing what your deal breakers are can be helpful if and when you start dating again. Put them on paper and understand the "whys" behind them.

breathe. slowly. deeply.

(38) Good Grief

Another term for grief is "pain." If you repress, ignore, or numb pain by self-medicating—it's going to stay trapped inside and cause problems down the road. Moving through the grief phases is the key to healing the pain associated with this breakup. Don't be surprised if you go back and visit a grief phase. Maybe you get through the denial, anger, bargaining, and depression phases. But out of nowhere, you're back in the anger phase. It's alright. Feel it and work through it, as there are bound to be messages that anger will give you . . . about YOU.

You'll hit an upward turn at some point. You'll be able to say, "Yeah, that breakup was very hard, but you know, I've learned a lot about myself, others, and life. And, these lessons make me a better person for me, but also for someone else down the road should I want another relationship." Don't rush. Make this "in between" time sacred. Stay on this self-directed healing journey.

Today, write a letter to you from your guardian angel, who absolutely adores you. This angel is your "person"—the one you can trust with your very life. They are so very proud of you. You're the one they cherish time with. Try to really feel their feelings about you as you write. Use affirmation, praise, encouragement, compliments, motivation, and inspiration. When you're done, read the letter out loud to yourself. And, keep it handy for the days you need that extra encouragement.

my light is always shining

(38) Good Grief

the sun will come out...tomorrow!

(39) You, Profiled

Here is your chance to "profile" yourself. Today, take some time to profile yourself, but only put positive qualities down. You can list them or even better, write a paragraph or two. Even if you don't fully feel the positive qualities just yet, write them down anyway. (You'll get there.)

For example: "I am a kind, funny, ambitious person who enjoys the simple things in life. I am honest, easygoing, courteous, and have integrity. People tell me I make them laugh, and it's true. Not many people know this about me, but I am quite sensitive. I have a real heart to help ease people's suffering. Three things I'm super proud of is the fact that I have a generous heart, I can listen to people well, and I never give up."

Write as much as you want. If you need keyword ideas, Google "positive character traits." Refer back to this on those days you need a boost.

i understand the value of step by step

(40) Who Do You See?

Today is about "mirror work." Take about a minute and look in your eyes in a mirror. Soften your eyes as you keep your gaze. If a minute feels too long, look as long as you'd like. Notice what kinds of thoughts and sensations are occurring in your mind and body.

Do you feel emotions? If so, what are they? Where do you feel them in your body? Stomach? Chest? Are you criticizing yourself? If so, how? Does this make you feel seen? Silly? More self-aware?

Mirror work is a powerful tool that can help you see past the surface stuff and see straight into your spirit—which is precious and radiant! It can also reflect back to you how you're truly feeling about yourself, and if it's negative, you have an opportunity to change that to positive. Take time to really see you!

i am my own super-hero

I am courageously dreaming up a beautiful life.

(41) My Attachment Style

What is your Attachment Style? (Anxious? Secure? Avoidant? A mixture of Anxious and Avoidant?) Hopefully, you've already done some research and learned what style you identify with.

Now, write down some of the core wounds associated with that style. For example, if you identify Anxious Attachment Style, some core wounds may be:

- *I will be abandoned.*
- *I am unseen and/or unheard.*
- *I am not good enough.*
- *I am unworthy.*

Think of your core wounds as like the center of an onion. Over the years, you may have accumulated other negative beliefs/emotions that layered on top of that center. (Life sucks, I'll never be happy, I am bad, etc.) When you've identified some core wounds (shadow work can help), it's time to acknowledge and recognize that these beliefs are NOT TRUE. They are false and by you identifying them and calling them out, you're applying light to the dark, so to speak. Because the truth is that under the "core" of that onion, you are luminous energy.

{There's more writing room on the next page.}

i am not my masks

(41) My Attachment Style

i value feeling safe and secure

(42) Life Vision

Take some time today to write about how you want to see your life go in terms of career, friendships, growth, health, finances, and spirituality.

Paint a picture of your ideal life. As you write, feel the positive emotions as if this kind of life is already here. Embody them. Relax your eyes, smile, and dream up the exact kind of life you desire!

As you do, God, Spirit, or whatever your higher power is will be orchestrating behind the scenes on your behalf. Trust the process.

i am doing great at being uniquely me

(43) Me, Empowered

You are stepping more and more into your empowered self. You're doing the inner work that needs done to feel, heal wounds, and integrate shadows.

You are owning your wholeness. Your inherent goodness and pureness.

How does this make you feel? What specific emotions are arising within you? If you're feel artsy today, draw a picture of YOU, empowered.

If drawing is not your thing, close your eyes and visualize YOU, empowered. (Capes are acceptable.)

i am brave

(44) Dedicated To Authentic Love

Picture yourself five, ten, or twenty years older looking back at yourself now. You see that you're dedicated to learning about self-love and relationship love on a whole new level.

Write a letter from your future self to your present self. Write it in the space of knowing that you're making the effort. You're doing what you need to do to heal and grow. You've chosen to live a mindful life dedicated to self-love, God-love, and other-love.

What would your older self want to say to encourage and support you?

i am living mindfully

(45) And So It Is

As we near the end of the journal, focus on courageously dreaming the kind of life you truly desire.

Today, write a short story in the present tense of the kind of life you truly desire. Be specific. There's no right or wrong here. Take a deep, slow breath, relax, and just start writing.

For example: *"My life is amazing! I feel more at peace than I've ever felt before. I am grateful. I wake up each morning knowing I am creating the kind of life I truly desire. I'm getting to know myself at a deep level and this feels good. I'm more confident. I'm optimistic. Life is not perfect, but that's alright. When rough patches come along, I'm not drowning in fight, flight, or freeze mode. I'm living mindfully, in expectation of goodness. And so it is!"*

i am evolving

the past can teach
such valuable lessons.

open your heart.
let it remain pliable.

pain may come,
but it can also go.

we can release it
bit by bit,
layer by layer.

trust the process.

(46) One Step Back, Three Steps Forward

Today, I want you to look back through your journal starting from Day 1. As you reread your entries, note anything that jumps out at you.

Do you see your progress? Can you see any patterns? Do you think you're getting through the grief process?

Can you guess what stage you're in now? (No right or wrong.)

Once you review your journal entries, write about how you're feeling compared to Day 1. Also, write about some lessons you have learned thus far on your healing journey.

i love and approve of myself

(47) Onward, With Hope and Self-Love

Jot down some notes on how you're going to continue your healing journey. Making a solid plan will certainly help you out down the road.

Will you continue to journal? Do you have a couple books on your "read" list that you can get into that will encourage you?

Check out the suggestions at the end of this book.

Do you have a solid support system? (friends, family, therapist, support group, community, etc.)

i am leaning on my support system

(48) What If I Don't Feel Better?

Maybe you've gone through this journal and you're still struggling. That's understandable. Not everyone progresses along the healing journey at the same pace. And, quite honestly, there are some things you may be working on "healing" well into the future—even in a future relationship.

In fact, relationships are fertile soil for nurturing healing on all levels. The following phrase adopted from a Twelve-Step group helps me a lot: "Think progress; not perfection." **You ARE making progress.** You ARE taking time and making the effort to heal, grow, evolve, and simply show up in the world more secure, with a more healthy, mature love for self and others.

That's something to pat yourself on the back about. Write about the progress you have made since the ended relationship and life in general. Brainstorm and jot down your accomplishments, Aha moments, revelations, insights, etc.

i am after progress; not perfection

(49) On a Positive Note

Here's an opportunity to show your poetry and/or short story writing skills. Don't worry. There's no right or wrong here. Today, take some time to create a poem or short story using as many of the following words as you can. See if you can embody the positive words as you create. You may even want to copy your creation onto a notecard or piece of paper and place it in a spot that you see daily. Remind yourself of just how incredible you truly are.

Adorable, amazing, authentic, balanced, beautiful, blessed, calm, celebrate, centered, cheery, compassionate, connected, conscious, consistent, courageous, delightful, determined, fabulous, flourishing, free, genuine, glad, growing, happy, honest, hopeful, insightful, incredible, joy, love, lovable, luminous, openhearted, passionate, peace, powerful, proactive, radiant, relaxed, resourceful, responsible, safe, secure, sincere, strong, terrific, unique, valuable, worthy

{There's more writing room on the next page.}

i am an amazing person

(49) On a Positive Note

so proud of myself

(50) Celebrate Your Progress

Take a deep breath, slowly exhale, and relax into the beautiful soul that you are. Today, think about how you want to celebrate you, your progress along your life journey thus far, and your hope for a secure, happy, harmonious future. This is a milestone celebration that you will anchor with a ritual or ceremony of your choice.

- You're showing up and doing your inner healing work.
- You've committed to a life marked with self-love and self-care.
- You've embraced vulnerability, authenticity, and support when needed.
- You're moving through obstacles, tough emotions, disappointments, and more.
- You're showing up more present; more empowered. That's worth celebrating!

Ritual/ceremony ideas:

- Create a sacred altar where you place items that remind you of love, peace, joy, higher power, etc. (gems, pictures, statues, etc.)
- Have a celebration dinner with family/friends
- Expressive dance (Dance it out!)
- Prayer, meditation
- Nature walk
- Journal
- Write a poem
- Paint a picture

{There's more writing room on the next page.}

(50) Celebrate Your Progress

i choose to live mindful & smile more

Standing For Your Joy

First, let me congratulate you on completing the journaling prompts in this book. I hope you were able to give yourself big doses of self-love and compassion. I also hope you are seeing just how resilient and expansive your heart truly is.

And even though it may have felt broken, the **truest part of the heart** is untouchable by "ended relationship wounds". This is the spiritual part that bleeds medicine for a lifetime of accumulated pain.

The part that is always nudging you to keep trying. Keep going. Keep believing.

Getting over a breakup is certainly no easy feat. I don't have to tell you that. However, your willingness to do some digging, reflect, contemplate, etc., tells me that you're quite courageous and wise.

So, thank you for showing up for yourself in such a sacred way. My hope is that you've gotten to know yourself better as you progressed through this journal. I hope that by journeying through the "tough stuff", you are gaining insight and lessons that you can use for a lifetime.

Now, keep going, dear one, using faith and your inner emotional GPS system to lead you to better spaces and places.

Drop down and lean in. Listen to what's going on under the surface. Feel, deal, and heal. And don't just feel the tough stuff. Feel the good too!

Feel the way you DESIRE to feel, even if you have to fake it till you make it for now. Because you are healing and transforming yourself one day at a time. As you make the effort, you are unleashing powers that will help you stand tall and embody yourself as sovereign, sacred spirit.

Should you be completely healed now that you've finished this journal?

While that would be wonderful, it's more likely that you're still on the healing journey. You may have made it through the roughest parts, but there may be some tough days that come.

Let's not forget that healing doesn't usually happen in a linear fashion. It's more like a zig-zagging road with some ups and downs. But you're navigating the path, and that sure counts for something.

There were times after a breakup I thought I'd NEVER feel better or be able to move on.

But I did, and thankfully I had friends that would remind me of that every so often. And you will feel better and move on too, in your timing and in your unique way.

While I'm truly sorry you had to experience such pain after a breakup, use the pain as a springboard for powerful lessons and growth – mentally, emotionally, physically, and spiritually.

You will make it.

You will thrive.

You can and will embody more and more the peace and joy you desire.

You are worthy, lovable, and loved.

In great gratitude for you,

About the Author

Dominica Applegate is a gentle soul showing up in this world to help others heal, grow, and evolve. She's especially interested in using her experiences and her story to encourage others.

For over ten years, she's reached thousands of people globally with her inspirational writings about waking up, doing inner healing work, creating healthier relationships and enjoying a more meaningful life.

Professionally, she's equipped with a graduate degree in counseling and over ten years' experience working in the mental health field. Personally, she's been a serious seeker since her late teens, immersing herself in various spiritual practices.

Her books include:

- *Into the Wild Shadow Work Journal: Reclaim Your Wholeness*

- *Goodbye Codependency: A 40-Day Devotional And Guided Journal To Boost Self-Care*

- *The Pain, It Shapes Her World.* {Collection of Poetry}

Her interests include ancient wisdom, transpersonal psychology, psychobiology, attachment theory, and conscious evolution.

Learn more at rediscoveringsacredness.com

Helpful Books

The following are some additional resources that may help you navigate this time in your life, as well as relationships in general.

- *The Journey from Abandonment to Healing: Surviving Through and Recovering from the Five Stages That Accompany the Loss of Love* by Susan Anderson

- *Getting Past Your Breakup: How to Turn a Devastating Loss into the Best Thing That Ever Happened to You* by Susan J. Elliott

- *Keeping the Love You Find: A Personal Guide* by Ph.D. Harville Hendrix

- *Embracing the Beloved: Relationship as a Path of Awakening* by Stephen Levine

Attachment Styles

- *Wired for Dating: How Understanding Neurobiology and Attachment Style Can Help You Find Your Ideal Mate* {Audiobook} by Stan Tatkin

- *Wired for Love: How Understanding Your Partner's Brain and Attachment Style Can Help You Defuse Conflict and Build a Secure Relationship* by Stan Tatkin

Shadow Work

- *The Dark Side of the Light Chasers: Reclaiming Your Power, Creativity, Brilliance, and Dreams* by Debbie Ford

- *Owning Your Own Shadow: Understanding the Dark Side of the Psyche* by Robert A. Johnson

- *Into The Wild Shadow Work Journal: Reclaim Your Wholeness* by Dominica Applegate

Printed in Great Britain
by Amazon